Contents

Any words appearing in bold, **like this**, are explained in the Glossary.

Was your pet once wild?

You may think that you just have a pet hamster, but the hamsters people keep as pets are very close to their wild relatives. Finding out more about the wild side of your pet will help you give it a better life.

*Did you know that hamsters belong to the same family as mice and rats? They are all **rodents**. This means they have big front teeth called incisors that keep growing all their lives.*

There are many different types of hamster living in the wild.

4

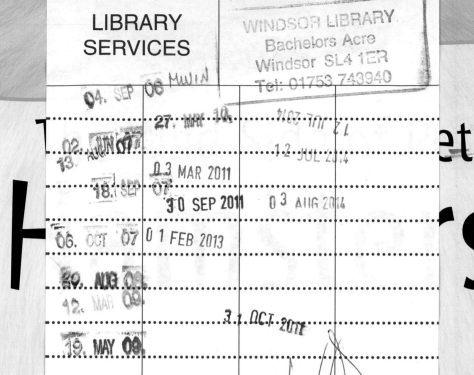

www.raintreepublishers.co.uk
Visit our website to find out more information about **Raintree** books.

To order:
☎ Phone 44 (0) 1865 888112
📄 Send a fax to 44 (0) 1865 314091
💻 Visit the Raintree Bookshop at **www.raintreepublishers.co.uk** to browse our catalogue and order online.

First published in Great Britain by Raintree,
Halley Court, Jordan Hill, Oxford OX2 8EJ,
part of Harcourt Education.
Raintree is a registered trademark of Harcourt
Education Ltd.

Editorial: Melanie Copland and Sarah Chappelow
Design: Richard Parker and Tinstar Design Ltd
    (www.tinstar.co.uk)
Illustrations: Jeff Edwards
Picture Research: Mica Brancic and
    Charlotte Lippmann
Production: Duncan Gilbert

Originated by Ambassador Litho Ltd
Printed and bound in China by South China
Printing Company

10 digit ISBN 1 8444 3933 X (hardback)
13 digit ISBN 978 1 8444 3933 1 (hardback)
09 08 07 06 05
10 9 8 7 6 5 4 3 2 1

10 digit ISBN 1 8444 3939 9 (paperback)
13 digit ISBN 978 1 8444 3939 3 (paperback)
10 09 08 07 06
10 9 8 7 6 5 4 3 2 1

**British Library Cataloguing in
Publication Data**
Waters, Jo
The Wild Side of Pet Hamsters
636.9'356
A full catalogue record for this book is available
from the British Library.

Acknowledgements
The publishers would like to thank the following
for permission to reproduce photographs: Ardea
p. 4 (Duncan Usher), 5 (Kenneth W. Fink), 7
(John Daniels), 9 (Johan de Meester), 11 (John
Daniels); FLPA pp. 6, 21, 26; Getty Images pp.
5 (Photodisc) 26 (Photodisc); Harcourt
Education Ltd/Tudor Photography pp. 5, 14,
15, 16, 19, 20, 23, 29; Minden Pictures pp.
10, 22, 27, 28 (Heidi & Hans-Juergen Koch);
Nature Picture Library p. 24 (Ingo Arndt), 25.

Cover photograph of a hamster in its nest
reproduced with permission of NHPA (Ernie
Jones). Inset photograph of a Roborovski's
hamster reproduced with permission of NHPA
(Daniel Heuclin).

The publishers would like to thank Michaela
Miller for her assistance in the preparation of this
book.

Every effort has been made to contact copyright
holders of any material reproduced in this book.
Any omissions will be rectified in subsequent
printings if notice is given to the publishers.

Hamsters can make good pets. They are small, so they do not take up a lot of room. They are fun and friendly pets if they are looked after properly.

Hamsters need everyday care, but this is part of the fun and responsibility of keeping a pet. Learning about your hamster can be very interesting.

Wild hamsters (top) and pet hamsters (bottom) are very similar.

Types of hamster

There are over 18 different types of hamster living in the wild. Common **species** include Syrian hamsters, Chinese hamsters, and Roborovski hamsters.

Hamsters can be very different sizes. A Syrian hamster is between 16 and 18 centimetres long (about 7 inches). A European hamster can grow to 32 centimetres (12 inches)!

Wild hamsters have **adapted** to their surroundings. Their coats are usually coloured to help them blend in.

These Chinese hamsters have stripes that make them hard to spot in grass.

Different breeds

Pet hamsters are similar to wild hamsters, but **breeders** have bred them specially to be pets. There are lots of different **breeds**. The most popular pet hamster is the Syrian hamster. It is also known as the golden or fancy hamster.

Russian hamsters may only grow to 10 centimetres (4 inches).

There are two other types of hamster that some people keep as pets. These are Russian hamsters and Chinese hamsters. They are less suitable pets as they can be quite shy and nervous. They have to be handled with care because their delicate bones get damaged easily.

Where are hamsters from?

The first wild hamsters came from deserts in Asia and Syria. Hamsters now live in Europe, Central Asia, Russia, Mongolia, and China.

Dwarf Campbells Russian hamsters live across central Asia, parts of Mongolia, and China. The dwarf Russian hamster lives in Kazakhstan and Siberia. The Chinese hamster and the Roborovski hamster live in China and Mongolia.

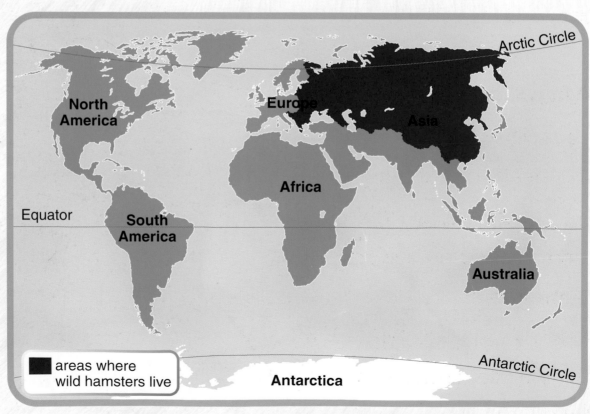

This map shows where wild hamsters can be found.

Choosing your pet

If you decide that a hamster is the right pet for you, you will need to find one. Always get your hamster from a good **breeder**. Never buy animals that have been caught from the wild, as this is cruel.

When you are choosing your hamster, make sure it is healthy. It should have bright eyes and be alert. It should have neat teeth and claws and a healthy coat and tail. Ask to handle the hamster to find out how tame it is.

Hamsters should not be sold until they are 5–8 weeks old.

Hamster habitats

Wild hamsters live in places like **steppes**. These are dry grassland areas. They also live in desert areas. They like sandy areas, such as dunes, best.

Hamsters burrow underground to make their homes. Sand dunes and dry earth are good places to burrow. They dig rooms for sleeping and others for storing food. Tunnels fan out from these rooms and join up the whole burrow.

Golden hamsters live in burrows.

Pet hamsters need a suitable cage to live in. As in the wild, they need a separate area in their cage for sleeping. This is called a nesting box.

Tunnels

Hamsters love cardboard tubes. They run through them as they would run through tunnels in the wild.

Wood shavings are the best bedding to use. Don't use pine or cedar wood shavings as they can make hamsters very ill.

A good cage will have a deep plastic base, a wire top and different levels for the hamster to move around.

11

Hamster anatomy

All hamsters have the same **anatomy**. They have round, solid bodies and short legs. Their front feet have four toes and their rear feet have five toes.

Hamsters have oval heads and large front teeth for **gnawing** and eating. They have short, round ears and a short tail.

Different **species** of hamster look different. A Chinese hamster is slim and small, but a European hamster is much fatter and bigger.

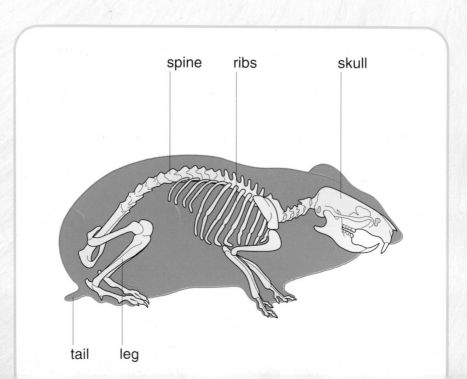

spine   ribs   skull

tail   leg

This drawing shows the skeleton of a hamster.

How to pick up a hamster
Be careful, as hamsters move quickly and don't like being handled roughly. Gently scoop the hamster up in both hands and don't squeeze it too tightly.

Pet hamsters have the same anatomy as wild hamsters. But **breeders** have bred pet hamsters specially to make them look different. There are lots of different types of coat. Some hamsters are semi-**albino**, which means they have red eyes and white fur, but black ears. Rex hamsters have a curly coat.

Senses

Hamsters have very sensitive senses. But they rely mostly on smell and hearing.

Wild hamsters use their superb hearing to avoid **predators**. They also use it to listen out for other hamsters.

Hamsters use their sense of smell to find food. They have a special **gland** on their sides which makes a smelly substance. They rub this on things to leave a **scent** mark to mark their **territory**. Other hamsters can smell this.

Hamsters do not have very good eyesight.

Pet hamsters use the same senses as their wild relatives. They don't have very good eyesight. They can be easily frightened if you move too suddenly near them.

Pet hamsters also have a good sense of smell. If your hand smells of food when you pick up your hamster, it may think your finger is food and have a nibble! Wash your hands first.

Hamsters use their whiskers for feeling their way in tunnels and dark places.

Movement

Hamsters use their muscles to move around. They are very active animals. Their short legs and solid bodies are good for living in tunnels and squeezing through tight spaces. They also climb and they use their short tails to help them balance.

Some hamsters, like Chinese or Roborovski hamsters, can run very quickly.

Swimming

European hamsters are good swimmers. They even **inflate** their cheek pouches to help them stay afloat!

In the wild, hamsters can run fast to escape predators.

Exercising

Pet hamsters also use their short legs to run and jump. They can be quite difficult to catch!

Chinese hamsters are very good climbers. They use their claws to cling on to things. They will cling on tightly to your fingers if you pick them up.

Hamsters need plenty of exercise. They should be able to move around a lot in their cage. Different levels are good for this.

If your hamster has a wheel, make sure it is a solid one. Hamsters can trap their legs in wheels with rungs.

What do hamsters eat?

Wild hamsters eat **grains** like oats and barley. They will also nibble plants and grasses. Sometimes they eat roots, berries, and fruits.

Hamsters have pouches on both sides of their mouths. They use them to carry food and bedding. Syrian hamsters can store up to half their own body weight of grain in their cheeks!

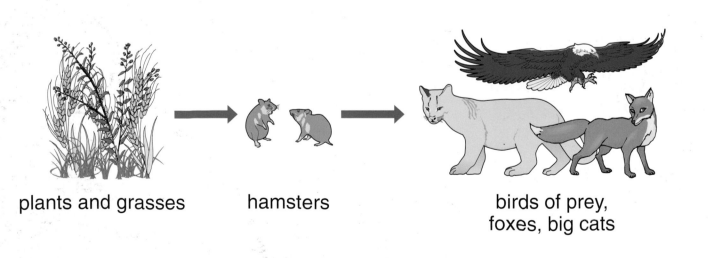

| plants and grasses | hamsters | birds of prey, foxes, big cats |

Hamsters fit into a **food chain** like this.

Pet hamsters cannot search for food as they would in the wild, so you must feed them the correct **diet**. You can get dry mix at pet shops.

Bad foods

Never feed onion, raw potatoes, kidney beans, or rhubarb to hamsters. These things are poisonous to them.

Your hamster should always have a fresh supply of clean water. A water dropper bottle is the best way to give water.

Hamsters should always have a fresh supply of dry mix, but they also enjoy fruit, vegetables, and dandelions.

Foraging and playing

Wild hamsters are very active. They can spend hours each night searching for food. They are **herbivores** so they do not need to hunt for their food. But they do have to **forage** for fresh grass and plants.

Wild hamster babies play together, and some adults will play-fight. Playing is part of learning what to do when they get older.

In the wild, hamsters carry food back to their burrow in their pouches.

Natural feeding

You can make feeding time more like it would be in the wild. Scatter your hamster's food over the cage floor and let it forage.

A hamster can get lots of exercise in a ball and have fun too!

Pet hamsters enjoy playing with toys. You can buy toys like balls, ladders, and tunnels.

Hamster balls are a good way of letting your hamster out in the house. The hamster can run around and explore, but cannot escape. Always take the hamster out if it looks tired or anxious. Make sure it can't roll off the edge of tables or down stairs.

Do hamsters live in groups?

In the wild, some **species** of hamster live in groups and are quite **sociable**. **Dwarf** Campbells Russian hamsters are happiest living in pairs or small groups. Winter dwarf Russian, Roborovski, and Chinese hamsters like to live in **colonies** and are very sociable animals.

Living alone
Syrian, Turkish, and European hamsters are **solitary** *animals. When they get to about 8–10 weeks old, they go off to live on their own. They will fight with other hamsters and guard their* **territory** *fiercely.*

Sometimes hamster burrows can get a bit crowded!

Just like wild hamsters, some pet hamsters like company, but others prefer to live alone. Make sure you find out which type your pet hamster is. If you put two Syrian hamsters together in a cage, they will fight.

Other types of hamster, such as dwarf hamsters and Chinese hamsters, prefer living in a pair or a group.

If hamsters haven't grown up together, introduce them slowly. Watch them carefully to make sure they get on.

Sleeping

Wild hamsters all need to sleep. They sleep in their burrows. Hamsters are **nocturnal** animals. This means they are most active at night and sleep during the day.

Hamsters go into a very deep type of sleep called **hibernation**. They hibernate between October and March, when the temperature drops below 8 °C. They only wake up every 5 or 6 days to eat and drink.

This hamster is going to hibernate in its cosy nest.

Just like their wild relatives, pet hamsters are nocturnal. They spend most of the day curled up in their nests. The best time to play with your hamster is when it wakes up in the evening.

In the wild, hamsters build comfortable nests in their burrows. Pet hamsters need to do this in their cages. Give them some soft paper to line their nests with. Do not use wool or fluff as this can get tangled around their legs.

You should not disturb your pet when it is asleep.

Life cycle of hamsters

Different **species** of hamster live for different lengths of time. Most hamsters, including Russian, Syrian, and Chinese hamsters, live for between 2 and 3 years. The bigger European hamster can live for up to 8 years.

Most hamsters are fully grown and able to **breed** by the time they are 8-10 weeks old.

This European hamster has a litter of 6 pups.

Female hamsters are called does and males are called bucks. The babies are called pups.

Hamsters breed very easily. They can produce a litter of 6–8 pups several times a year. That's a lot of hamsters! Make sure you keep males and females apart to stop them breeding. If they do breed, you will have to find good homes for all the babies.

Pups cannot see or hear when they are born.

Common problems

In the wild, hamsters are often eaten by **predators**. They do not have any defences and the only thing they can do is stay hidden.

Wild hamsters can suffer if their **habitat** is damaged or destroyed.

Drought
Drought is when there is not enough rain. Wild hamsters live in naturally dry areas. If there is less rain than usual, the plants will not grow and the hamsters may starve.

Wild hamsters will fight with any hamster that comes into their **territory**. Sometimes they can kill each other.

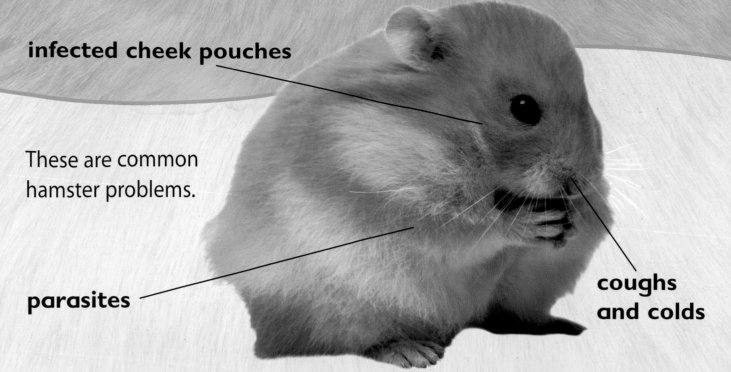

infected cheek pouches

These are common hamster problems.

parasites

coughs and colds

Itches and sneezes

Hamsters can get **parasites**. These include fleas, mites, or ticks on their skin. Your vet can give you something to treat them.

Hamsters can become ill from infected cheek pouches. This happens when sharp or sticky food has got stuck in their pouches. Get your vet to treat this immediately.

Hamsters can also get coughs and colds. This can be serious, so always check with your vet.

Now you know more about why hamsters behave the way they do, you can look forward to a rewarding future with your pets.

Find out for yourself

A good owner will always want to learn more about keeping pet hamsters. To find out more information about hamsters, you can look in other books and on the Internet.

Books to read

Hamster (How to look after your pet… series), Mark Evans. Dorling Kindersley, 1996

A Pet's Life – Hamsters, Anita Ganeri, Heinemann Library, 2004

Using the Internet

Explore the Internet to find out about hamsters. Websites can change, so if one of the links below no longer works, don't worry. Use a search engine, such as *www.yahooligans.com* or *www.internet4kids.com*. You could try searching using the key words 'hamster', 'pet', and 'wild hamsters'.

Websites

A good site for finding out about hamster care can be found at: *http://www.hamsters.co.uk* or *http://www.petwebsite.com/hamsters.asp*

The website of the National Hamster Council has lots of useful information: *http://www.hamsters-uk.org*

Disclaimer
All the Internet addresses (URLs) given in this book were valid at the time of going to press. However, due to the dynamic nature of the Internet, some addresses may have changed, or sites may have ceased to exist since publication. While the author and publishers regret any inconvenience this may cause readers, no responsibility for any such changes can be accepted by either the author or the publishers.

Glossary

adapt become used to living in certain conditions

albino having no colour in skin or fur, with white fur and pink eyes

anatomy how the body is made

breed when two animals mate and have babies. A breed is also a particular type of animal within a species.

breeder someone who raises animals

colonies large groups of animals living together

diet what an animal eats

dwarf a small type of an animal

food chain the links between different animals that feed on each other

forage to search for plants and food to eat

gland small organ of the body

gnawing chewing, biting, or nibbling at something

grains cereals like oats, wheat, or barley

habitat where an animal or plant lives

herbivores animal that only eats plants

hibernate to go into a special deep sleep when it is cold

inflate to blow up with air

nocturnal awake at night

parasites tiny animals that live in or on another animal and feed off it

predator animal that hunts and eats other animals

rodents a group of small animals with teeth that keep growing all their lives

scent another word for smell

sociable likes company and living in groups

solitary the opposite of sociable – likes to live alone

species similar animals that can have babies together

steppes areas of cold, dry grassland

territory/territorial the area where an animal hunts and lives. An animal will protect its territory fiercely.

Index